CHARLIE BROWN'S 'CYCLOPEDIA

Super Questions and Answers and Amazing Facts

Featuring
What We Wear

Volume 11

Based on the Charles M. Schulz Characters

Funk & Wagnalls, Inc.

Photograph and Illustration Credits: The Bettmann Archive, Inc., 520, 521; © British Crown, photo used by permission of Her Britannic Majesty's Stationery Office, 498 (top); British Tourist Authority, 519; David G. Brown, 523 (bottom); Paul Cedfeldt, 496 (right); Anne Miller Christensen, 505 (top), 549; Colonial Williamsburg Photograph, 486; Jack Drake/Black Star, ix; Eleanor Ehrhardt, 485, 497 (bottom left); Will Faller/Boy Scouts of America, 496 (bottom left); Terry Flanagan, 487, 497 (middle right); Marc Gave, 489 ("Lucy's Loom"); Greek National Tourist Organization, 519 (inset); Japanese National Tourist Organization, 504; Light Opera of Manhattan, William Mount-Burke, producer/director, 499; Charles R. Luchsinger, 496 (top left), 497 (top right, middle left, bottom right); The Metropolitan Museum of Art, Bequest of Bashford Dean, 1929, 494; The Metropolitan Museum of Art, Gift of William H. Riggs, 1913, and Fletcher Fund, 1921, 493; The Metropolitan Museum of Art, Rogers Fund, 1906, 483 (top); Museum of the American Indian, Heye Foundation, 490, 491, 492, 523 (top); National Aeronautics and Space Administration, xi; The New-York Historical Society, 515 (bottom); Smithsonian Institution, Picture Collection of the Cooper-Hewitt Museum Library, 500, 515 (top), 526; Amidou Thiam, 483 (bottom); UNICEF, 502 (bottom); UNICEF/Water/Satyar, 502 (top); United Nations, 501 (top); United Nations/AID/Purcell, 501 (bottom); United Nations/J.P. Laffont, 505 (bottom); United States Navy, 495, 497 (top left); © Martin Weaver/Woodfin Camp & Associates, 510, 511.

Introduction

Welcome to volume 11 of *Charlie Brown's 'Cyclopedia*! Have you ever wondered who invented cloth, or what a hoop skirt is, or what clothes will look like in the future? Charlie Brown and the rest of the *Peanuts* gang are here to help you find the answers to these questions and many more about what we wear. Have fun!

Clothing Around the World
Yesterday and Today

Why do people wear clothes?

For many reasons. The most important one is protection. Winter clothes help protect people from the cold. Raincoats and boots keep them dry in rainy weather. Shoes protect their feet against hard rocks or hot sidewalks.

Most people are shy about showing their bodies to everyone around them.

People also wear clothes to tell others something about themselves. Some clothes show what a person does for a living. Police officers, nurses, and airline pilots, for example, wear uniforms to work.

The customs of different countries set fashions for clothes. In the United States brides wear white at weddings. In China brides wear red. Because of customs, people all over the world dress up in special clothes for holidays.

Dressing up helps people pretend. They may wear costumes and masks when they put on a play.

Last but not least, people wear clothes to help them look better.

What did the first clothes look like?

They were pieces of cloth or fur. People wrapped them around their waists, the way you wrap yourself in a towel. You've probably seen pictures of cave men dressed this way. To keep warm, people long ago wrapped other pieces of fur or cloth over their shoulders.

Another early form of clothing was the tunic (TOO-nik). People in Central Asia were wearing tunics 5,000 years ago.

What is a tunic?

A tunic is a long shirt that is made of two pieces of fur or cloth. One piece is for the front and one is for the back. The pieces are sewn together at the shoulders and at the sides.

Tunics can be long or short. In ancient Greece, more than 2,500 years ago, men wore tunics just above their knees. Women's tunics reached to the ground.

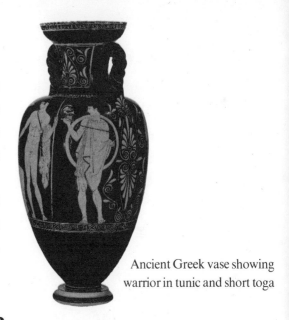
Ancient Greek vase showing warrior in tunic and short toga

Did the ancient Greeks wear underwear?

A poor person in ancient Greece had only one tunic—which was both underwear and outerwear. A richer person wore a tunic as underwear. Over the tunic, a rich Greek wore a himation (hih-MAT-ee-on), or toga.

What is a toga?

A toga is a large piece of cloth worn over one or both shoulders. Togas were popular for many hundreds of years in ancient Greece and Rome. During that time, toga styles changed a lot. But an ordinary man's toga was much smaller than a rich man's toga. A rich man wore his toga draped around his body many times. An ordinary man draped his only once.

Toga-like clothing is a style today in some parts of the world, especially Africa.

Woman from Senegal wearing togalike cloth over her shoulders

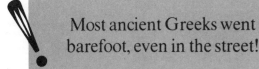

Most ancient Greeks went barefoot, even in the street!

When did men start wearing pants?

The first pants we know about for sure were worn 2,500 years ago in Persia (now Iran). Both men and women in ancient Persia wore pants.

The Persians traded with people from Central Asia. The Central Asians were nomads, people without settled homes. They lived in tents and moved from camp to camp. These nomads also wore pants. Today, no one is sure if the Persians copied the style from the nomads, or if the nomads copied the style from the Persians!

Who invented cloth?

No one knows. We do know that 5,000 years ago Africans were already making cloth from tree bark. Before Columbus discovered America, American Indians were also making bark cloth. It is possible that other people may have made cloth before either of these did.

To make bark cloth, both the Africans and the Indians laid wet pieces of bark across each other. Then they pounded the bark with rocks. The tiny fibers—hairlike pieces—that made up the bark stuck together. They formed a piece of cloth. West Africans still make bark cloth this way.

484

Who invented thread?

Thread is made naturally by worms, insects, and spiders. The first human thread-makers probably got the idea for spinning thread from one of those creatures.

What is spinning?

Spinning is a way of twisting many short hairlike pieces called fibers together into one long thread.

How is spinning done?

For hundreds of years, people used a spinning wheel to make thread. It could spin only one thread at a time. Today modern factories use huge machines to spin hundreds of threads at a time. Here's how a thread is made.

The fibers are placed in a straight line. The end of each fiber overlaps the beginning of the next fiber. When the fibers are twisted, they cling together. The more the fibers overlap, the stronger the thread. Extra fibers can be twisted in to make the thread thicker.

What plant fibers are good for thread?

Any tall, stringy plant can be used to make thread. You can make thread yourself from tall grasses or cattails. Hang the plants in a cool, dry place for two or three weeks. They will become very dry. Then carefully pull apart the fibers and braid or twist them into thread.

Flax, hemp, and cotton are three plants grown for their fibers. From flax fibers we make linen. From hemp fibers we produce rope. From cotton fibers we make cotton cloth.

What animal fibers can be used for thread?

Thread can be made from the hair of any animal. People in ancient Asia used the hair of sheep, camels, and goats. Early South Americans used wool from wild mountain animals, such as llamas (LAH-muz), vicuñas (vye-KOO-nyuhz), and alpacas. These three goatlike animals still live in the Andes Mountains of South America.

North American Indians used horsehair, buffalo fur, and moose hair for thread making.

ISN'T THAT INTERESTING, SNOOPY? THEY CAN MAKE THREAD FROM DOG HAIR...

KLUNK!!

SUCH INSENSITIVITY BOGGLES THE MIND...

Could you make thread from your dog's hair?

You could if you had enough of it. But you'd need a lot of hair to spin enough for a piece of cloth. When your dog is shedding, you might sweep up the hairs and try it. But your dog would be VERY UNHAPPY if you tried it at any other time!

Indians in the American Northwest raised herds of dogs for their fur.

Who discovered how to make cloth from thread?

Probably fishermen in Egypt 5,000 years ago. They made fishnets by knotting and tying threads together. Nets were probably the first "cloth" made from thread.

MY GRATITUDE TO THE WEAVER OF MY SECURITY BLANKET KNOWS NO BOUNDS...

Who invented weaving?

We don't really know. Weaving is a special way of putting together threads to make cloth. The process may have been discovered by net makers. Net makers tied the ends of their threads around weights. The weights kept the threads from getting tangled. The weights also made the threads hang tight and straight while the men were working. That probably gave someone the idea for a loom.

488

What is a loom?

A loom is a machine for weaving. The loom keeps a whole row of threads tight and straight. The worker can then pass another thread in and out of the straightened threads.

People in Egypt were weaving more than 5,000 years ago!

Where did prehistoric people get needles for sewing?

Before metal was discovered, people carved needles from wood and bone. People that lived near the sea used fish bones and bits of shell. People in deserts used cactus spines.

Europeans were using metal needles about 2,500 years ago. Most American Indians did not have metal tools before the European settlers came to America just a few hundred years ago.

Where did American Indians get beads to decorate their clothes?

From the European settlers. Tiny beads for decoration were made in European glass factories. The Indians traded furs and blankets for the bright beads. They liked to sew the beads onto their clothes and weave them into their belts. Today beadwork is one of the best-known American Indian crafts.

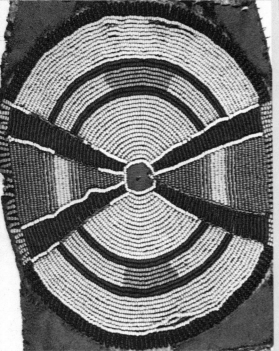

Detail of beading

Moccasins

What did American Indians wear before the settlers came?

Many Indian men and women wore leather tunics. They wore soft leather shoes called moccasins. In cold weather, they put on leggings—pieces of fur or leather which they wrapped around their legs. The leggings came up over their knees, like long socks.

How did American Indian styles change after the settlers came?

After meeting European women, Indian women in the northeast began wearing skirts and blouses. The fashion of cloth shirts spread among northeastern Indian men. In the southwest, Indian lands were settled by people from Spain. Spanish men wore long pants made of cloth. Soon the Indian men began to wear cloth pants, too.

490

Did the settlers get any styles from the Indians?

Yes. Daniel Boone and other pioneers dressed much like the Indians did. They wore long leather tunics, leggings, and moccasins. Their fur capes and leather bags copied Indian styles, too.

Leggings

Buckskin dress in tunic style

DON'T KNOCK IT TILL YOU TRY IT...

Indians and early settlers sometimes kept their feet warm in winter by stuffing the toes of their moccasins with grass!

What do Indians wear today?

Most American Indians wear the same kinds of clothes as other Americans. But for special ceremonies the Indians dress up in their traditional clothing.

491

Feather headdress

How did an Indian chief keep his war bonnet on during a battle?

He didn't have to—he didn't wear it! Its many feathers would just have been in the way! War bonnets were for special feasts and ceremonies. They were called war bonnets because the feathers and other decorations on them were prizes given for special deeds in war.

CAN I HELP IT
IF THEY'RE MA
OF FEATHERS?

What did the Indians wear in battle?

Some Indians fought in armor. Armor is a hard covering that protects a person in battle. The northwestern Indians made chest armor from thin strips of wood and leather. Around a warrior's neck was a wooden collar. It covered his chin and mouth, too. On his hair and forehead he wore a carved wooden helmet. It was in the form of either a fierce-looking person or an animal. The human face was supposed to scare the enemy. The animal face was supposed to bring the warrior good luck. The wood protected the man from clubs and arrows.

Other Indians fought bare-chested. They protected their chests with shields. A shield is a flat piece of armor that a warrior carries on his arm. Indian shields were often made of buffalo skins. The skins were dried to make them strong and hard.

Wooden helmet in shape of eagle

492

When did soldiers start wearing metal armor?

About 3,500 years ago. At that time soldiers in the Middle Eastern countries of Assyria (uh-SIHR-ee-uh) and Babylon (BAB-uh-lun) sewed small pieces of metal to their leather tunics. The metal gave warriors extra protection against enemy arrows. About 2,500 years ago the Greeks wore large pieces of metal on their chests and backs. They also wore metal helmets.

Much later, about 600 years ago, some soldiers in Europe called knights began to wear full suits of armor. A suit of armor covered a soldier's whole body with large pieces of metal joined together. The armor had hinges at the knees and the elbows. A heavy metal helmet covered the soldier's face, head, and neck.

WHY DO I LET HIM TALK ME INTO THESE THINGS?...

How could knights move around in all that armor?

Not very easily! Young knights had to train themselves to carry the extra weight. But their horses had the biggest burden. They carried the knights AND the armor. Often a knight's horse wore armor, too. Then the horse had to carry even more weight.

WHEN THEY TALK ABOUT THE GOOD OLD DAYS, I DON'T THINK THIS IS WHAT THEY HAVE IN MIND...

Armor for horse and man

493

What did ordinary soldiers wear?

Until 400 years ago, most common soldiers wore leather tunics and helmets. Sometimes the leather was covered with small pieces of metal. In some countries common soldiers wore chain mail under their tunics. Since their tunics had no sleeves, only chain mail covered their arms.

Some knights wore chain mail, too. But they wore it under a metal chest plate.

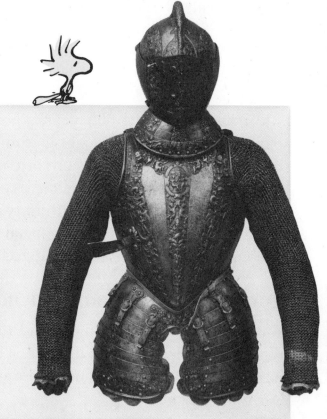

Did they get chain mail at the post office?

No. A soldier who wanted chain mail would visit the blacksmith's shop. Chain mail was a cloth made of small metal chains linked together. It protected the wearer from spears and arrows.

Once there were two mice who lived in a museum.

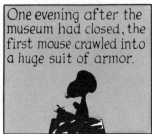

One evening after the museum had closed, the first mouse crawled into a huge suit of armor.

Before he knew it, he was lost. "Help!" he shouted to his friend.

"Help me make it through the knight!"

What do modern soldiers wear?

Soldiers now wear cloth uniforms. The color and style of the uniform show what country a soldier comes from. They also show in what branch of the armed services he or she is. The uniforms are sometimes decorated with buttons and bright patches.

494

SNOOPY, OL' PAL, MAYBE WE CAN BRING BACK THAT OLD STYLE AGAIN...

In the 1600s in Europe, people slashed up their clothes to be in style. They copied this fashion from soldiers whose clothes had been torn in battle!

United States Marines   *Insets*: Parachutist's Insignia; Navy Cross Medal

What do the patches on soldiers' uniforms mean?

Some patches tell a soldier's rank—how important that person is in the armed services. A beginning soldier might wear a patch with one stripe. A long-time soldier might wear a patch with eight or nine stripes. The uniforms of officers have metal bars and stars. A "four-star general" is one of the most important officers in the army.

Medals and patches also show what the soldier has done. Soldiers get medals for bravery and good service.

495

Do children wear uniforms?

Yes. Scouts wear uniforms. In most countries children wear uniforms to school. In the United States children who go to public schools don't wear uniforms. But many children in private schools do.

Are there other kinds of uniforms?

Yes. Here are some pictures of people wearing clothing that shows what kind of work they do.

Veterinarian

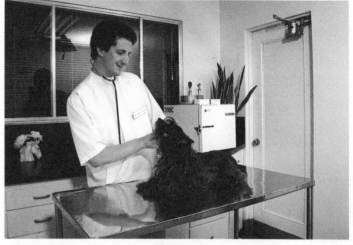

Navy crewman

Chef

Pilot

Minister

Maître d' (MAY ter DEE)

497

Why do cooks wear tall white hats?

Cooks have been wearing white hats since at least 600 years ago. Back then most European workers wore special clothes as signs of their jobs. Bakers and cooks wore short, puffy white hats. Styles in cooks' hats changed over the years. In the 1900s cooks started wearing tall white hats with puffs at the end. The tall white hat is now the sign of any restaurant cook.

The Imperial State Crown of England

Why do kings and queens wear crowns?

A crown sets a ruler apart from ordinary people. A crown is a symbol that stands for power. Each crown has a design that represents its own country. When a country crowns its rulers, it gives them power over the country.

Kings and queens don't wear crowns all the time. Crowns are only for special ceremonies. Many crowns are heavy with gold and jewels. No person can wear one for more than a few minutes without getting a headache.

Some of the clothes of King Henry VIII (the Eighth) of England had so many jewels sewn on them that no cloth showed through!

King Henry VIII

498

Why do lawyers and judges in England wear white wigs?

The English lawyer's wig is a style left over from 300 years ago. At that time all important men in England wore wigs. The wigs had long curls that came down over the men's shoulders. Wig styles changed around the year 1700. The new style had hair pulled back in a ponytail. But lawyers and judges kept the older-style wigs as a sign of the importance of the law.

I CAN HEAR MY MOTHER NOW..."GET A HAIRCUT, SON..."

Performer wearing wig

In the 1790s it was the style for men to put powder on their wigs.
Some wigs were powdered white.
Other wigs were light pink, silver, or blue!

CLAP CLAP CLAP CLAP

THE COURT JESTER...

WHY CAN'T I HAVE A NORMAL DOG LIKE EVERYONE ELSE?...

PAWPET THEATER
The Foolish King
NOW PLAYING
EXCITING!
TERRIFYING!

Is it true that George Washington wore a wig?

No. People often say he did because wigs were in style for important men at the time of the American Revolution. Although many of the men who founded the United States wore wigs, Washington always wore only his own hair. He powdered it and pulled it back in a ponytail.

Hair styles worn by rich women in the 1770s were almost 3 feet high!

Do people still wear wigs?

Yes, many people do, often because they have lost their own hair. Modern wigs are supposed to look as much like real hair as possible.

Why do women in some countries wear veils?

Veils are supposed to keep men from looking at women. This custom is very old. Women were wearing veils in a Middle Eastern country called Ur 5,000 years ago.

A few religions forbid women to show their faces. Some women who belong to the Moslem faith cover every part of their bodies except their eyes.

Veiled women in Morocco

Do any men wear veils?

Yes. Among the Tuareg (TWAH-reg) people of the Sahara desert, all men cover their faces. Women go without veils. Tuareg men believe they are more important than people who are not Tuareg. Ordinary people may not see their special faces.

 Tuareg men wear their veils even when they eat and drink!

501

Veiled African man

What else do people in the Sahara Desert wear?

Tuareg people wear sandals with big, wide soles shaped like paddles. The wide soles keep their feet from sinking into the sand.

They also wear what most desert people wear—loose clothes. Loose clothes allow air to reach a person's body easily. The air helps to keep the body cool in hot weather. Some desert people dress in long, flowing robes. Others wear loose shirts and trousers.

Desert dwellers protect their heads from the sun by covering them with cloth. Some desert men wrap their heads in turbans.

What is a turban?

A turban is a long piece of cloth that is wound around a person's head. Men wear turbans in Egypt, India, Arabia, and some other Asian and African countries. In some African countries, women wear turbans.

How do you get a turban to stay on your head?

Wrapping a turban is like tying a huge knot, with your head at the center. You pass the ends of the turban over and under each other. Then you tuck the ends of the turban under the folds of cloth.

There are hundreds of different ways to wrap a turban. The way one is wrapped sometimes shows what tribe or family a man comes from.

Turbans are sometimes fastened with a jeweled pin.

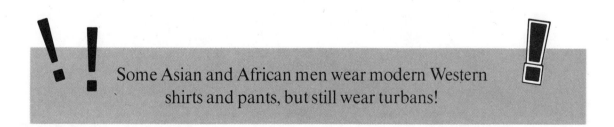

Some Asian and African men wear modern Western shirts and pants, but still wear turbans!

What do we mean by "Western" clothing?

By Western clothing we don't mean clothes that are worn back home on the range. We mean clothing styles that come from modern Europe or America.

Western clothes are shirts, dresses, pants, and skirts. Today these clothes are worn by people all over the world.

Even in Eastern countries such as Japan, most people wear Western clothes for everyday use. The native clothes, such as kimonos (kuh-MOE-nuhz) are now worn mostly on special occasions.

Kimonos

What is a kimono?

The kimono is the traditional dress of the Japanese people. It is a long robe with wide sleeves and a wide sash. Both men and women wear kimonos.

Do Chinese people wear kimonos?

No. The kimono is a Japanese style. The Chinese used to wear robes, but they were different from kimonos—how different depended upon the part of China in which they were worn. Some Chinese robes had narrow sleeves and collars. Some had wide sleeves and no collars. Some had belts and others didn't. Some were worn over pants or skirts, and others were worn alone.

Performer wearing Chinese robe

Indian women wearing saris

What is a sari?

A sari is a long piece of cloth that women in India, Bangladesh, and nearby countries wear as a dress. It is usually made of silk or some other thin material.

Before dressing in a sari, a woman puts on a short blouse and a half-slip. Then she tucks one end of the sari into the top of the half-slip. She wraps the cloth around her body a few times and throws the other end over her shoulder. The bottom of the sari reaches to the floor.

505

What is a sarong?

A sarong is a long piece of cloth that is wrapped around the body once. Men and women who live on islands in the Pacific Ocean wear sarongs. So do some people of Southeast Asia. Men wrap their sarongs around their waists. Women wrap theirs under their arms.

Some people in Africa wear clothes that look very much like sarongs.

What is a muumuu?

Some women in Hawaii wear long, loose cotton dresses called muumuus (MOO-mooz). The style began when European and American settlers arrived in Hawaii in the 1800s. The newcomers thought that the Hawaiian women weren't wearing enough clothes. So they made the women cover up with muumuus.

507

What do Eastern people wear on their feet?

Most people in China, Japan, and other east Asian countries wear Western shoes. In other words, their shoes are much like yours. But sandals made of rope or straw are popular.

One style of Japanese sandal is the géta (GEH-tah). It has a very thick wooden sole called a "platform." Most gétas are only a few inches high. But when Emperor Hirohito (hear-o-HEE-toe) was crowned in 1926, he wore gétas almost a foot high!

In cold places such as Tibet and Mongolia, people wear boots of fur or heavy cloth.

People who live on the Pacific Islands often go barefoot. The weather is warm, and there are no hard, paved streets. So they have little need for shoes.

 About 300 years ago, some European women wore shoes with platforms up to 30 inches (76 centimeters) high!

What do African people wear on their feet?

What they wear on their feet depends on where they live and how much money they have. Jungle dwellers need no shoes and go barefoot. Other Africans, too poor to buy shoes, also go barefoot. Some people can afford sandals. And in African cities, many people wear Western-style shoes. Much the same is true in South America.

Who invented raincoats?

Raincoats were probably invented by soldiers, shepherds, and other people who had to spend a lot of time outside in bad weather.

Cloaks were the first rainwear. A cloak was just a flat piece of leather or heavy cloth. Its owner may have rubbed animal fat into the leather to make it waterproof. When rain began to come down, he simply threw the cloak over his head.

What did cowboys wear when it rained?

In the days of the Old West, cowboys wore huge hats with wide brims. Cowboys and other ranch workers still wear them today. These hats are their main protection against rain, hail, snow, and sun.

Why do cowboys and cowgirls wear scarves around their necks?

The scarves that they wear are called bandannas. An old cowhand, J. Frank Dobie, once made a list of the uses of a bandanna. Here is the list:

1. Keeping the sun off the back of the neck.
2. Covering the nose on a dusty day.
3. Wrapping the ears in cold weather.
4. Tying on the hat in windy weather.
5. Blindfolding horses.
6. Wrapping a cut or wound.
7. Making a sling for a broken arm.
8. Straining mud out of stream water.
9. Covering the face of a dead cowboy.
10. Hanging horse thieves.

Today ranch hands probably use their bandannas for pretty much the same things—except, perhaps, hanging horse thieves!

Where did cowboy styles come from?

Cowboy styles came to North America from Spain. The Spaniards brought cattle with them. They also brought cattlemen. Spanish cattlemen wore wide leather hats called sombreros (some-BRAY-roes). They also wore leather vests, leather boots with metal spurs, and leather chaps.

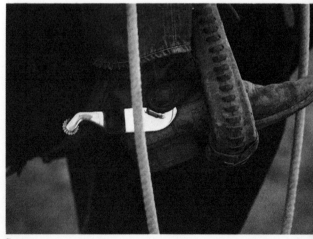

Spur

What are chaps?

Chaps are heavy leg coverings that are worn on the outside of jeans or pants. They are made of tough leather. They protect the cowhand's legs from thorns and from cold when he or she is out riding a horse.

Cowboy in chaps

Do modern ranch workers wear chaps?

Yes, but North American ranch workers wear chaps less today than they used to. These people don't ride on horseback as much now as they did before. They often use cars instead. But in Argentina and Venezuela, two South American countries, there are many cowboys who do their work in the old-fashioned way. They still ride horses every day. So they need chaps.

Why do cowboys and cowgirls wear high-heeled boots?

High heels keep the feet of anyone on a horse from slipping out of the stirrups. If their feet aren't in the stirrups, riders can easily fall off their horses.

511

What other clothes did old-time cowhands wear?

When cowboys were working, they dressed in shirts and heavy work pants. Sometimes they put on an extra shirt to keep warm. Cowboys did not usually wear jackets on the job. They said jackets made their arms too hard to move. Instead they often wore vests.

Modern cowhands still wear the same kind of work clothes that old-time cowboys did.

When a cowboy of the 1850s or 1860s was finished with his work and had been paid, he often bought himself a new suit of clothes. Then he dressed in the latest style. No one could tell he was a cowboy.

What clothes were in style for men in the Old West?

Some men in the Old West copied the eastern styles. Men in eastern cities wore suits that had matching long pants and jackets. With the suits they put on fancy silk or velvet vests. They also wore white shirts, bow ties, and tall black hats called top hats.

Other men in the West dressed in fancy Indian-style clothes. Wild Bill Hickock, a famous frontier scout and marshal, was known for his fancy clothes. He wore Indian tunics of soft leather embroidered with beads. He carried silver guns with ivory handles.

What did women in the Old West wear?

A pioneer woman usually had only one good dress for going to church and to parties. The rest of the time she wore a blouse and a long cotton skirt. Sometimes in cold weather pioneer women wore leather leggings, like Indian women did.

Pioneer women also tried to keep up with the latest styles from back east. These included the newest fashions in bonnets and shawls. One popular style about 100 years ago was the very full skirt. Some of the skirts were so wide they couldn't fit through doors!

How did women get their skirts to be so full?

At first women made their skirts stand out by wearing many petticoats at once. But it was hard for women to get around that way. Their clothes weighed too much. So women started wearing hoop skirts to lessen the weight.

What is a hoop skirt?

A hoop skirt was a petticoat that looked like a cage. A woman wore her hoop skirt under a dress or skirt. The skirt covered the "cage." The hoop skirt held the skirt out much like a metal frame supports a lampshade. Some hoop skirts folded up when the woman sat down.

Since huge skirts got in the way, why did women wear them?

Because they wanted to be stylish. People have worn many very silly and uncomfortable styles over the years simply because they were in fashion.

What was probably the most uncomfortable style ever?

The hourglass waist. From the 1840s until the early 1900s people thought that beautiful women should have the shape of an hourglass. This means that they had to be very small in the middle and wide above and below that. Women wore either very full skirts or bustles. A bustle was a puff of cloth at the back of a skirt. It was often held up by a wire hoop. The hoop collapsed when the woman sat down. Women's waists were pulled in very tight with underwear belts called corsets.

A girl began tightening her waist when she was about 14. Every morning she put on her corset—even if she was playing tennis that day! As the girl grew older, her corset was laced tighter and tighter. It kept her waistline from growing. A few women's waists were only 12 or 14 inches around! Most modern women have waists at least 10 inches larger than that.

Dress with a bustle

In the 1890s some five-year-old girls wore corsets!

LET'S HEAR IT FOR TODAY'S LIBERATED WOMAN...

Wasn't it hard for women to breathe in tight corsets?

It certainly was. Corsets were both uncomfortable and unhealthy. That is why women began to talk about wearing more comfortable clothes. In 1850 Amelia Bloomer tried to get women to wear shorter dresses and roomy trousers—without corsets. People laughed at her idea. They called her trousers "bloomers." But Mrs. Bloomer won in the long run. About 50 years later, women got tired of not being able to move around. They started to wear simpler, looser clothes.

Amelia Bloomer wearing bloomers

515

Is it true that women used to wear bathing suits with long pants?

Yes. In fact, in the 1850s and 1860s, women wore to the beach wool suits with long pants, full skirts, and high collars. And on their feet they wore canvas bathing slippers! If all that clothing got wet, it became very heavy. Anyone who tried to swim would sink!

Little by little, bathing suits got smaller and smaller. About 90 years later the bikini was invented. That barely covered up anything!

In most parts of the world, people always swam without ANY clothes on.

516

What did old-time bathing suits for men look like?

Most men didn't wear bathing suits at all until about the 1850s. At that time men and women started going to the beach together. At first the men wore just bathing trunks. But by the 1870s people were becoming more modest. So the men covered up with knitted tops that were like T-shirts. Their trunks reached to the tops of their knees. This style lasted for about 50 years.

When did women start wearing pants?

In many countries of the world, pants have been part of women's clothing for hundreds of years. But in Europe and the United States pants for women were not considered proper until the 1920s. Even the pants women wore as part of their bathing suits were mostly covered by their skirts.

Movie stars helped make pants popular in America. The stars wore loose pajamas of shiny materials for lounging at home or on the beach. By the 1930s women were wearing pants for sports and to parties as well.

While we were fighting World War II—from 1941 to 1945—many women worked in factories. They replaced men who had gone to war. The women factory workers wore overalls and other men's clothes. By the time the war ended, women were used to the comfort of pants. They began wearing pants more and more often. But until the 1960s most stores and offices did not allow women to wear pants to work. Now most women may wear pants whenever and wherever they like. Some schools still insist that girls wear skirts to class.

Do any Western men wear skirts?

Most Western men wear pants. But in a few countries men sometimes wear skirts. Their skirt styles are usually ones that have been worn in their countries for many hundreds of years.

For special occasions some Scottish men dress in knee-length skirts called kilts. Kilts are woven in brightly colored plaids. Each Scottish plaid belongs to a different family, or clan.

The guards at the Greek parliament building also wear kilts. The Greek kilts are white.

Have men ever worn silly styles?

Yes. At various times, men have worn huge capes, very long feathers in hats, and tight starched collars. One of the silliest men's styles of recent times was the zoot suit. It was popular with some American men in the 1930s and 40s. The style called for a baggy jacket that reached to the knees and baggy pants that came up to the chest. The suit was usually dark-colored with thin light stripes. With it, men often wore a long chain that hung from the chest nearly to the floor. They usually put on suspenders to hold up the pants. And they topped off their outfit with a floppy hat.

 Men in the 1600s wore high-heeled shoes and silk stockings trimmed with bows and laces!

Are there people who don't wear any clothes at all?

Only a very few of the world's people go naked. These live in isolated parts of Australia, South America, and Africa. They belong to tribes that have not met many people from other places.

But even those who wear no clothes decorate their bodies. Some people in South America and Africa paint their bodies in bright designs. Others dress up for special occasions in colorful jewelry.

When did people begin wearing masks?

More than 10,000 years ago, cave people in Europe wore animal masks. Before a hunt, they held special dances. They believed the dances would help them have a good hunt. They wore masks to the dance. Some masks were of the animals the men were going to hunt. Other masks were of the gods in which the people believed.

The ancient Greeks wore masks on the stage 2,500 years ago. They put on plays in honor of their gods.

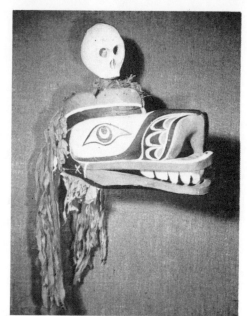

Indian wooden wolf mask

Have ordinary people ever worn masks on the street?

The ancient Greeks and Romans had masked holidays. On those days people would dress in costumes and masks. They would dance and play music in the streets. Masked holidays were great fun. With covered faces, people could go anywhere and do anything they liked. No one knew who they were.

The Greek and Roman holidays were much like the Mardi Gras (MAR-dee-grah) today. A Mardi Gras is held every winter in New Orleans. Another takes place in Rio de Janeiro, Brazil. People wear funny costumes and masks in the streets.

Of course, as all trick-or-treaters know, children wear masks in the streets every year on Halloween.

Performers wearing masks in festival in Nepal

Do people ever wear masks in everyday life?

Masks are worn for many sports. Skiers sometimes wear knitted wool masks. The masks are like socks, with holes for the skiers' eyes, nose, and mouth.

Divers wear masks underwater. Baseball catchers wear masks made of metal and leather. Bank robbers wear masks, too.

Why do catchers wear masks?

Catchers wear masks to protect their faces. When the batter hits a foul ball, the ball can come right at the catcher's face. A fast baseball can badly hurt someone who gets hit in the face with it.

524

Why do some athletes wear shoulder pads?

Football is a very rough game. The padding protects the players if they get hit or knocked down. Hockey players also wear padding to protect them from falls.

Do people wear padding in ordinary clothes?

Yes. Jackets and coats are often padded in the shoulders. In the 1940s stylish women's jackets had big pads in the shoulders. The pads made their shoulders look wider.

When did Western men start wearing jackets?

The modern jacket came into use in England on December 15, 1660. Before then Englishmen wore short capes. They copied the style from the French and bought many capes made in France.

King Charles II (the Second) of England wanted his people to stop buying clothes from France. So on December 15, 1660, he appeared in court dressed in a Turkish-style jacket. He knew that everyone would copy his style and give up French capes.

The King of France was angry at Charles's fashion change. To get even, he made all the servants in the French court wear jackets.

When did long pants come into fashion for men?

Around 1800. Before that time, long pants were worn only by common work-ingmen. Rich men wore knee-length pants over stockings.

In 1789 a revolution began in France. The common people overthrew their rich rulers. After that no one wanted to look rich. All men began wearing long pants, which were ordinary working clothes.

 The zipper did not become popular until 1931! Before that, people fastened their clothes with buttons and hooks.

OH, YOU HANDSOME DOG, YOU!

Why do styles change?

In the past, people copied the clothes of the kings, queens, and people of the court. And some styles changed by royal order, as in the case of jackets in France.

Sometimes styles have changed after two different groups of people met. One copied the other. In colonial America, settlers and Indians traded styles. Today people all over the world copy styles from the United States. Blue jeans, T-shirts, and tennis shoes are a few of the imitated fashions.

Styles are also set by the people who design, make, and sell clothes. Ordinary people would not buy new clothes as often as they do if styles did not change.

What will clothes look like in the future?

We don't know exactly what styles people will wear. Fashion changes in strange ways. But in the future we may wear fewer clothes. We probably won't need heavy winter coats. Scientists in the space program have invented new types of cloth. One type is a warm, lightweight cloth used for astronauts' clothes. Even now, raincoats and other clothes are made with various kinds of cloth invented by the space program.

Some clothes in the future will probably be "unisex" clothes. That means both men and women can wear them. Jeans and T-shirts are some of the "unisex" clothes that people wear today.

Skin-divers must have special clothes in order to keep warm under water. They wear skin-tight outfits called wet suits that are made of rubber with lots of bubbles in it. The air in the bubbles helps divers float. A face mask helps divers see under water. They wear fins on their feet to help them swim faster.

Skin-divers

As recently as 200 years ago, most boys in Western countries wore full-length skirts until they were about six years old!

WHAT?

I'M TRYING TO IMAGINE YOU WEARING A FULL-LENGTH SKIRT.

IT'S HARD TO TELL WHAT PIG-PEN IS WEARING!

MY DOG, THE NONCONFORMIST!

In the 1850s Levi Strauss began making heavy brown pants for the local gold miners in San Francisco. But Strauss soon began dyeing the pants deep blue, and called them blue jeans.

Astronauts need special clothing to help them survive in space. The astronauts who visited the moon wore long underwear lined with plastic tubes filled with water to help keep them cool. Over the underwear was a pressurized suit made up of six layers of special nylon, rubber, and fiberglass fabrics. Finally, a ten-layer suit was worn on top of that for lunar surface walks. A tough plastic helmet protected the heads of the astronauts. Special visors screened the sun's most dangerous rays from their eyes. Heavy gloves made of metal fabric protected their hands. Their feet were protected with plastic lunar overshoes that had 33 layers of insulation. The astronauts carried life-support systems on their backs that supplied oxygen, cooling water, suit pressure, and radio communication. On earth the whole outfit weighed 183 pounds. But in the moon's weak gravity it weighed about 30 pounds.

Astronaut practicing lunar maneuvers on earth